EXPLORING SPACE

TELESCOPES

BY DALTON RAINS

WWW.APEXEDITIONS.COM

Copyright © 2024 by Apex Editions, Mendota Heights, MN 55120. All rights reserved. No part of this book may be reproduced or utilized in any form or by any means without written permission from the publisher.

Apex is distributed by North Star Editions:
sales@northstareditions.com | 888-417-0195

Produced for Apex by Red Line Editorial.

Photographs ©: Dima Zel/NASA, cover; Shutterstock Images, 1, 7, 14–15, 29; Bill Ingalls/NASA, 4–5; Alex Evers/Northrop Grumman/NASA, 6; ESA/CSA/STScI/NASA, 8–9, 22–23, 24–25; Photo 12/Universal Images Group/Getty Images, 10–11; Library of Congress, 12–13; NASA, 16–17, 18; G. Illingworth, D. Magee, P. Oesch, R. Bouwens, HUDF09 Team/ESA/NASA, 19; S. Beckwith and Hubble Heritage Team/ESA/NSA, 20–21; Martin Bernetti/AFP/Getty Images, 26–27

Library of Congress Control Number: 2023910081

ISBN
978-1-63738-743-6 (hardcover)
978-1-63738-786-3 (paperback)
978-1-63738-871-6 (ebook pdf)
978-1-63738-829-7 (hosted ebook)

Printed in the United States of America
Mankato, MN
012024

NOTE TO PARENTS AND EDUCATORS

Apex books are designed to build literacy skills in striving readers. Exciting, high-interest content attracts and holds readers' attention. The text is carefully leveled to allow students to achieve success quickly. Additional features, such as bolded glossary words for difficult terms, help build comprehension.

TABLE OF CONTENTS

CHAPTER 1
WEBB 4

CHAPTER 2
HISTORY OF TELESCOPES 10

CHAPTER 3
SPACE TELESCOPES 16

CHAPTER 4
NEW TECH 22

COMPREHENSION QUESTIONS • 28
GLOSSARY • 30
TO LEARN MORE • 31
ABOUT THE AUTHOR • 31
INDEX • 32

CHAPTER 1

A rocket blasts off into space. It carries the James Webb Space Telescope. The telescope travels far from Earth.

The James Webb Space Telescope launched on December 25, 2021.

Webb's sunshield has five layers of fabric.

SUNSHIELD

The Sun's heat can cause problems. So, a few days after Webb launched, two robotic arms spread out shiny fabric. This fabric is called a sunshield. It keeps the telescope cool.

Webb begins to **orbit** the Sun. Scientists point its mirrors toward space. The telescope takes pictures of a huge **nebula**. It is very far away.

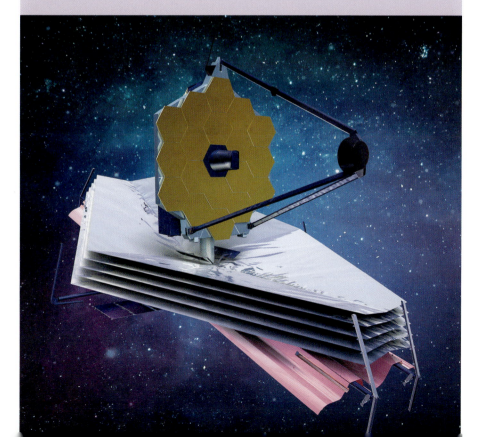

Webb began taking pictures about six months after launch.

Scientists pointed Webb at the Carina Nebula. They saw stars forming there.

Soon, a detailed image reaches Earth. Scientists can see the nebula up close. The image shows huge clouds of dust. Bright stars shine through the clouds.

FAST FACT

Webb mainly takes pictures in **infrared**. That lets it see stars inside clouds of dust.

CHAPTER 2

History of Telescopes

Telescopes are tools that make faraway objects seem close. At first, people made telescopes with lenses.

In 1608, Hans Lippershey made one of the first telescopes.

Galileo (left) was one of the first people to study space with a telescope.

In the early 1600s, scientists used telescopes to study space. They looked at the Moon and the planets. Later, scientists invented a new telescope. It used mirrors instead of lenses.

FAST FACT
Galileo discovered four moons orbiting Jupiter.

Bigger telescopes can see farther. So, scientists built huge **observatories**. They also used cameras. Pictures recorded what the telescopes saw. Computers helped sort the data.

In the 1990s, the Keck telescopes were built on a Hawaiian mountaintop. They were the largest telescopes on Earth.

LOCATION MATTERS

Earth's **atmosphere** bends light that passes through it. That's why the tops of mountains are good spots for telescopes. The atmosphere is thinner higher up.

CHAPTER 3

SPACE TELESCOPES

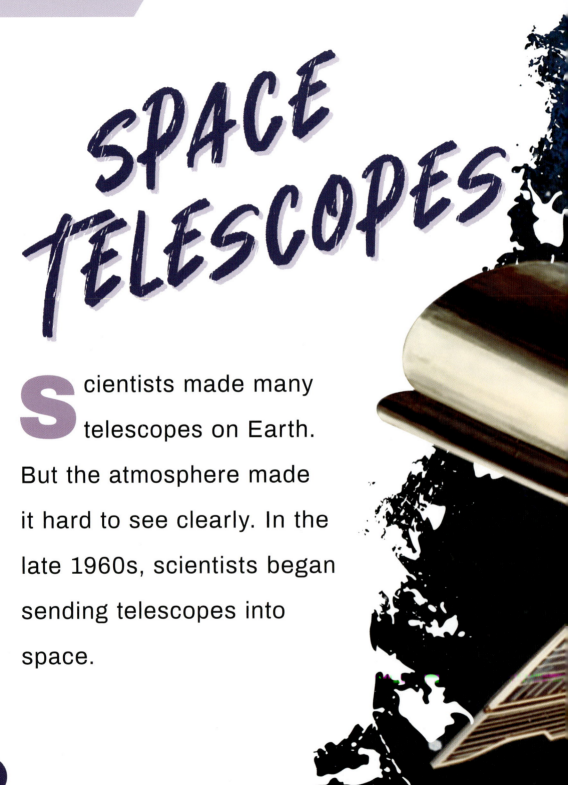

Scientists made many telescopes on Earth. But the atmosphere made it hard to see clearly. In the late 1960s, scientists began sending telescopes into space.

The first space telescope was called Stargazer.

The Hubble Space Telescope was an important project. It began to orbit Earth in 1990. Hubble took many pictures.

Hubble orbits 332 miles (535 km) above the surface of Earth.

In 1995, Hubble took a picture that showed thousands of different galaxies.

FAST FACT

At first, Hubble did not work properly. People had to fly to space and fix it.

Space telescopes helped make many discoveries. Scientists learned about different **galaxies**. They launched new space telescopes to learn even more.

DIFFERENT KINDS

Many telescopes observe light that humans can see. Others observe energy that people can't see. For example, some telescopes look at **X-rays**.

The Chandra X-ray Observatory studies X-ray light. Chandra's tools turn X-rays into visible images.

CHAPTER 4

NEW TECH

Space telescopes orbiting Earth could see a lot. But scientists wanted to learn even more. So, they sent the James Webb Space Telescope farther away.

Webb allowed scientists to see how nearby galaxies affect one another.

In 2023, Webb took a picture of a pair of stars in the process of forming.

Hubble mostly uses visible light. Webb mostly uses infrared. So, it can see more. Webb also uses a much larger mirror.

TIME TRAVEL

Light travels fast. But it does not move instantly. Some light takes billions of years to reach Earth. Telescopes look at it. They see what the **universe** looked like long ago.

Workers build parts of the Extremely Large Telescope in June 2022.

Scientists have many plans for the future. They hope to make even larger telescopes. They will discover more about the universe.

FAST FACT
In the 2010s, workers began building an observatory in Chile. It was called the Extremely Large Telescope.

COMPREHENSION QUESTIONS

Write your answers on a separate piece of paper.

1. Write a few sentences that explain the main ideas of Chapter 1.

2. Which telescope do you find most interesting? Why?

3. When was the first space telescope launched?
   - A. the 1600s
   - B. the 1960s
   - C. the 2020s

4. Why is a mountaintop a good place for a telescope?
   - A. There is no atmosphere there.
   - B. The atmosphere is thicker there, which bends more light.
   - C. The atmosphere is thinner there, which bends less light.

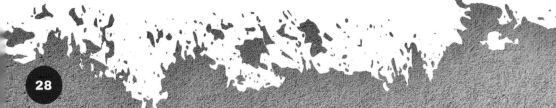

5. What does **detailed** mean in this book?

*Soon, a **detailed** image reaches Earth. Scientists can see the nebula up close. The image shows huge clouds of dust.*

    A. something that shows many features
    B. something that is very blurry
    C. something that has no color

6. What does **data** mean in this book?

*Pictures recorded what the telescopes saw. Computers helped sort the **data**.*

    A. computers that can work very quickly
    B. scientists who fix damaged telescopes
    C. information gathered to study something

Answer key on page 32.

GLOSSARY

atmosphere
The layer of air that surrounds Earth.

galaxies
Systems of many stars.

infrared
Invisible light rays that are longer than the rays that produce red light.

nebula
A cloud of gas and dust in outer space.

observatories
Rooms or buildings that have telescopes.

orbit
To follow a curved path around an object in space.

universe
Everything that exists.

X-rays
Invisible light rays that are shorter than the rays that produce visible light.

BOOKS

Corso, Phil. *How Do Telescopes Work?* New York: PowerKids Press, 2021.

Murray, Julie. *Telescopes*. Minneapolis: Abdo Publishing, 2020.

Peterson, Christy. *Cutting-Edge Hubble Telescope Data*. Minneapolis: Lerner Publications, 2020.

ONLINE RESOURCES

Visit **www.apexeditions.com** to find links and resources related to this title.

ABOUT THE AUTHOR

Dalton Rains is an author and editor from Saint Paul, Minnesota. He loves to learn about new science discoveries.

INDEX

E
Extremely Large Telescope, 27

G
galaxies, 20
Galileo, 13

H
Hubble Space Telescope, 18–19, 25

I
infrared, 9, 25

J
James Webb Space Telescope, 4, 6–7, 9, 22, 25
Jupiter, 13

M
Moon, 13

N
nebula, 7, 9

O
observatories, 14, 27

S
scientists, 7, 9, 13–14, 16, 20, 22, 26
Sun, 6–7

U
universe, 25–26

X
X-rays, 20

ANSWER KEY:
1. Answers will vary; 2. Answers will vary; 3. B; 4. C; 5. A; 6. C